Memo Devo 2.0: Memorization as Devotion

Published by Five Talents Audio
Copyright 2014 by Five Talents Audio
ISBN#: 978-0-9821616-9-2

Printed in the USA
ALL RIGHTS RESERVED
No part of this publication may be reproduced, stored in a retrieval system or transmitted in any form or by any means - electronic, mechanical, photocopying, recording or otherwise - without prior written permission.

Memo Devo 2.0

Memorization as Devotion: Volume 2

2nd Edition

"Sanctify them in the Truth. Your Word is Truth."
John 17:17

Steve Cook

Memo Devo 2.0

10 More Devotionals
Designed to Activate More Scripture in Your Life

Contents

Active Scripture Memorization 4
DIY Discipleship 5
A Simple Spirit 9
Worship 15
Heaven 21
My Body 27
Itching Ears 33
Death 40
Marriage 46
The Passover 55
Love, Part 2 66

ASM
Active Scripture Memorization

Wait a minute. Isn't that redundant?

I mean, isn't all Scripture supposed to be "living and active" already? (Heb4_12)

Ahh, yes, but it's not the Scripture that needs activating. It's the memorization.

For centuries, people have memorized and spoken back God's Word to each other in long form with powerful, reckless results for the Kingdom. In fact, up until about 500 years ago, it was our primary means of meditation, since most of us were illiterate.

But from the invention of that first printing press back in 1439 to the roll out of the latest iPhone, Bible memorization has slowly become a more text-based enterprise, usually done in isolation, with more personal goals in mind instead of as an act of worship. It is no longer the same active communal expression of love for Jesus that it was back in the 1st Century and therefore, I believe, we no longer experience all of its deepest spiritual benefits; benefits which Jesus Himself promised! (John 8:31-32, John 15:7-8, John17:17)

But what if we made a conscious effort to revive that experience? What if we re-introduced the radically ancient concept of **Active Scripture Memorization** back into our homes and churches? I believe we would see that the simple act of speaking back long memorized passages of Scripture to each other in community has the power to help transform our walk with Jesus. I believe we would experience better intimacy with God, a better witness for God, and better protection under God, all while using time and resources we already possess.

I believe one of the keys to 1st Century-style revival, is more 1st Century-style Bible study.

Steve Cook

DIY Discipleship
Matthew 28:18-20

Memo Devo 2.0
Matt28:18-20
Subject: DIY Discipleship

Day 1
Matt28:18

18 And Jesus came, and spoke to them, saying, "All POWER is given to Me, in Heaven, and on Earth."

This whole passage is familiar. Or is it? As I apply what I call the Tide Technique* and other mnemonic devices to each verse, the Spirit brings the truth of it to me as if it's all brand new, making it truly living and active, just as Jesus promises in Hebrews 4:12. It's really quite amazing!

While we usually do a verse a day in Memo Devo, we'll start out by taking the whole five days this week for just these three verses. It's a great passage to start with in a new Scripture memorization commitment.

Point To Ponder

My lone keyword in this verse is POWER. I build around and ponder that first. It is the starting place for any hope I may have of realizing Jesus' love in my life today. If I don't believe that one sentence first, I am going to have a hard time getting past the "clanging cymbal" stage of 1Cor13:1.

*More information on the Tide Technique can be found in tomorrow's Memo Devo and also at 5talentsaudio.com/tide.

Memo Devo 2.0
Matt28:18-20
Subject: DIY Discipleship

Day 2
Matt28:19

19 GO therefore, and TEACH all nations, BAPTIZING them in the Name of the Father, and the Son, and the Holy Spirit.

No mnemonic today, just three keywords to add to the one from Monday. Notice, VERBS usually work best as keywords. (except right then)

Now add verse 18*

18 And Jesus came, and spoke to them, saying, "All POWER is given to Me, in Heaven, and on Earth.
19 "GO, therefore, and TEACH all nations; BAPTIZING them in the Name of the Father, and the Son, and the Holy Spirit;"

*This is the basic idea behind the Tide Technique. Once I have solidified verse 19 in my short-term memory (by the way, I find that at least 10 repetitions of a verse is required to do that), I then "tide back", like water on a beach, to add verse 18. I do this slowly, adding one phrase at a time or however much I'm comfortable with, and always reciting to the very end of v19 each time. Biting off smaller chunks like this makes the process less overwhelming. It also gives me more confidence because I make it through successfully more often. Try it!

Memo Devo 2.0
Matt28:18-20
Subject: DIY Discipleship

Day 3
Matt28:20

20 TEACHING them to observe ALL THINGS, whatever I have commanded you. And lo, I am with you ALWAYS, to the end of the age. Amen.

Steve's Mnemonic: "All things. Always."

Jesus finishes His earthly ministry in Matthew by re-stating the great dual truth of the New Testament:

1) how He wants me to love Him (All things.)
2) how He wants to love me (Always.)

This also finishes our first week. Use the extra time to practice. New things are hard, I know. But you can do this. And remember to speak it back to someone. That's key! THAT'S Active Scripture Memorization: speaking back God's Word in community with other believers. Now that our toes are in the water, we'll dive a little deeper with a 5-Day Memo Devo from 1Corinthians next.

Put it Together Using the Tide Technique

18 And Jesus came, and spoke to them, saying, "All POWER is given to Me, in Heaven, and on Earth.
19 "GO, therefore, and TEACH all nations; BAPTIZING them in the Name of the Father, and the Son, and the Holy Spirit;
20 "TEACHING them to observe ALL THINGS, whatever I have commanded you. And lo, I am with you always, until the end of the age. Amen."

A Simple Spirit
1Corinthians 2:1-5

Memo Devo 2.0
1Corinthians 2:1-5
Subject: A Simple Spirit

Day 1
1Cor2:1

¹ And I, brothers, when I CAME to you, came not with excellency of WORDS or of WISDOM, showing you the testimony of GOD.

The subject of this verse, Paul's admission of his own technical inadequacy as a preacher, is quite frankly so compelling to me that all I need are those few keywords in CAPS to act as anchors and my brain will latch onto the rest using the Tide Technique*.

I like to apply those funny performance-based expressions of love we use in the church like "worship well" and "I'm so proud of..." to these five verses. It can be quite convicting. What if Paul spoke at my church? Would I listen to him? Or what if my Dad, who is a wonderful singer, sang at my church and messed up some of the notes, but someone still came up afterward and said how much his singing showed them the glory of God? Would I still be "proud" of him? The point is, I must always strive to be mindful of the Spirit at work, not myself. (Matt 5:16, Jeremiah 9:24, Isaiah 55:8-9)

*The Tide Technique is my means of textual memorization, using mnemonics and an unusual form of repetition. In this case, I would hide verse 1 in my short-term memory by repeating it out loud to myself at least 10 times. More on this tomorrow and at 5talentsaudio.com/tide

Memo Devo 2.0
1Corinthians 2:1-5
Subject: A Simple Spirit

Day 2
1Cor2:2

² For I DETERMINED not to know anything among you, except Jesus Christ and Him CRUCIFIED.

Paul gets right to the point. And it doesn't take an M.Div. to figure it out. The only manifestation of Christ's love that really matters is the true life He has given me.

Preach the Cross.

Put it Together Using the Tide Technique*

¹ And I, brothers, when I CAME to you, came not with excellency of WORDS, or of WISDOM, showing to you the testimony of God.
² For I DETERMINED not to know anything among you, except Jesus Christ and Him CRUCIFIED.

*After hiding verse 1 in my short-term memory by repeating it out loud to myself at least 10 times, I then do the same thing today with verse 2. After that, I begin to "tide back" slowly, like waves on a beach. First, I add the last phrase of v1 (or "...showing you the testimony of God.") and recite from there to the end of v2. Then I add the phrase before that, and so on, all the way back to the beginning. Remember to speak the words back to someone else. This is very important. But if that's not possible, I can at least run a long-term memory test by reciting while distracting myself with some simple task like folding laundry, yard work, driving or even juggling. Have fun and don't get discouraged. You can do this with the Spirit's help!

Memo Devo 2.0
1Corinthians 2:1-5
Subject: A Simple Spirit

Day 3
1Cor2:3

³ And I was among you in WEAKNESS, and in FEAR, and in much TREMBLING.

Paul re-phrases v1 to paint a very clear picture of what his preaching looked and sounded like to those without eyes and ears. Obviously, it's very encouraging to be able to identify with him in this way, right? But more importantly for me, he was obedient to do the thing that SCARED him the most in order to follow his true calling from Jesus. Remember he gave up the safe, "impressive" life of a Pharisee - a life he could be "proud" of; a life that certainly must have "seemed right" to the world(ly) around him; instead choosing to be disrespected, mocked and even pitied by his friends and peers. All for Jesus alone.

Put it Together Using the Tide Technique

¹ And I, brothers, when I CAME to you, came not with excellency of WORDS, or of WISDOM, showing to you the testimony of God.
² For I DETERMINED not to know anything among you, except Jesus Christ and Him CRUCIFIED.
³ And I was among you in WEAKNESS, and in FEAR, and in much TREMBLING.

Memo Devo 2.0
1Corinthians 2:1-5
Subject: A Simple Spirit

Day 4
1Cor2:4

⁴ Neither my WORD nor my preaching was in the enticing speech of man's WISDOM, but in demonstration of the Spirit and of power.

Steve's Mnemonic: Word Wisdom.

Just a simple alliteration today, but effective in helping trigger my brain to remember the rest of this verse in the process of short-term memorization.

While this verse looked to me at first like just another re-statement of v1, after pondering it a bit more, the Holy Spirit keeps bringing me back to that last phrase. Paul seems to be breaking down his message like a journalist would. The "How" it is delivered (v1,3), the "What" it is that gets delivered (v2), and "Who" must deliver it. He's always looking for opportunities to share the simple power of the Holy Spirit in his ministry. So inspiring!

Put it Together Using the Tide Technique

¹ And I, brothers, when I CAME to you, came not with excellency of WORDS, or of WISDOM, showing to you the testimony of God.
² For I DETERMINED not to know anything among you, except Jesus Christ and Him CRUCIFIED.
³ And I was among you in WEAKNESS, and in FEAR, and in much TREMBLING.
⁴ Neither my WORD nor my preaching was in the enticing speech of man's WISDOM, but in demonstration of the Spirit and of power.

Memo Devo 2.0
1Corinthians 2:1-5
Subject: A Simple Spirit

Day 5
1Cor2:5

⁵ So that your FAITH would not be in the WISDOM of man, but in the POWER of God.

Oswald Chambers once said, "Any Pharisee could have run circles around Mary doctrinally."

But she knew Jesus personally.

The best Bible teacher today is still the same one that Mary liked best. It's the one with supernatural power that surpasses even the most erudite mind ever conceived on Earth. And what's more, it's the one Who loves me beyond comprehension and is specifically tuned to my personality and needs at all times, enabling me in all circumstances. It is Jesus and His Spirit. But that's just too simple for me to buy. And Paul knew it would be. That's why the subject of this passage is more than just a sermon topic; it is a Mission Statement.

Put it Together Using the Tide Technique

¹ And I, brothers, when I CAME to you, came not with excellency of WORDS, or of WISDOM, showing to you the testimony of God.
² For I DETERMINED not to know anything among you, except Jesus Christ and Him CRUCIFIED.
³ And I was among you in WEAKNESS, and in FEAR, and in much TREMBLING.
⁴ Neither my WORD nor my preaching was in the enticing speech of man's WISDOM, but in demonstration of the Spirit and of power.
⁵ So that your FAITH would not be in the WISDOM of man, but in the POWER of God.

Worship
Psalm 100

Memo Devo 2.0
Psalm 100
Subject: Worship

Day 1
Ps100:1

[1] SHOUT joyfully to the LORD, all the Earth!

Steve's Mnemonic: "SHOUT first, ask questions later."

These first two verses of Psalm 100 basically answer the question, "What is worship?", about which volumes have been written. The KJV uses the phrase "Make a joyful shout..." and the Geneva uses "Sing loudly...". And while I have the utmost respect and admiration for those translations, here I think they reflect a somewhat more genteel (and quite frankly, a better-mannered) age, in which simply making a 'noise' or being 'loud' was much more conspicuous than it is today. And that, it seems to me, is the Author's first intention here. I must always seek to be CONSPICUOUS with my worship. God wants people to always *see* my love for Him first (Mark 12:30, Matthew 5:16) and then hopefully *ask* me why I have it (1Peter 3:15), especially in difficult circumstances.

Memo Devo 2.0
Psalm 100
Subject: Worship

Day 2
Ps100:2

² SERVE the Lord with gladness. Come before His courts with joyful SINGING.

Steve's Mnemonic: "Serve and Sing"

Now the other "worship shoe" drops on these first two verses of Psalm 100. The first verse answered "how" I am to worship – that is, as if sounding the "alarm" of God's love with my joyous heart. And this second verse tells me "when" I should sound that joyous alarm – namely, when I am serving and when I am singing – or ALL THE TIME.

I don't know about you, but that sure clears away a lot of the sniping and bickering I might be tempted to do over worship styles at church or how I'm being used by God today.

I have to say, this is already probably the clearest description of worship I have seen. And there's still three verses to go!

Put it Together Using the Tide Technique

¹ SHOUT joyfully to the Lord, all the Earth!
² SERVE the Lord with gladness. Come before His courts with joyous SONGS.

Memo Devo 2.0
Psalm 100
Subject: Worship

Day 3
Ps100:3

[3] KNOW that the Lord is God. It is He Who has MADE us, and not we ourselves. We are His PEOPLE, the sheep of His PASTURE.

You'd think I wouldn't still need reminding, but I have the same problem this Psalmist had, and the same one that Adam and Eve had. The minute I stop worshiping God, I begin worshiping myself... "as God, knowing good and evil." I fall for the same old lie that Satan has been telling everyone since Genesis 3 – a lie born of pride.

Btw, notice how the "shouting, serving and singing" parts of worship come before the "knowing" part. (Job 13:15)

Put it Together Using the Tide Technique*

[1] SHOUT joyfully to the Lord, all the earth!
[2] SERVE the Lord with gladness. Come before His courts with joyous SONGS.
[3] KNOW that the Lord is God. It is He Who has MADE us, and not we ourselves. We are His PEOPLE, the sheep of His PASTURE.

*As I repeat v3 out loud (about 10 times to start), my brain latches onto the keywords in CAPS and begins to finish out the phrases around them. I then "tide back" slowly, adding one phrase at a time, like waves on a beach, until I reach the beginning of the passage. It really is amazing how God has equipped our brains to do this.

Memo Devo 2.0
Psalm 100
Subject: Worship

Day 4
Ps100:4

⁴ Enter His gates with THANKSGIVING, and into His courts with PRAISE. Give THANKS to Him and BLESS His Name.

Up to now, this Psalm has been all about my worshiping God simply for Who He Is. The mere fact that He is God and I am here is reason enough for me to worship Him, and I should.

But now there's also something else to be specifically THANKFUL for as I worship. Something stated not just once, but twice (always a bit of a giveaway in the Bible as to its importance); something God certainly doesn't have to give me in order to deserve my worship, yet He does; something that ultimately makes any kind of relationship with Him possible at all.

What is this mysterious thing? Tune in tomorrow...(or you could just turn the page).

Put it Together Using the Tide Technique

¹ SHOUT joyfully to the Lord, all the earth!
² SERVE the Lord with gladness. Come before His courts with joyous SONGS.
³ KNOW that the Lord is God. It is He Who has MADE us, and not we ourselves. We are His PEOPLE, the sheep of His PASTURE.
⁴ Enter His gates with THANKSGIVING, and into His courts with PRAISE. Give THANKS to Him and BLESS His Name.

Memo Devo 2.0
Psalm 100
Subject: Worship

Day 5
Ps100:5

⁵ For the Lord is GOOD. His MERCY is eternal, and His FAITHFULNESS is from generation to generation.

Here the Psalmist lays out once and for all why my joy should never ever run dry, and why my worship should never wane, even if my fate on this earth is that of Job. (specifically, Job 1:13-2:10)

The Lord is God (v3) and the Lord is good.

What that means is that the only all-powerful being in existence is also all-loving, with my very best interests at heart, if I choose to access them. What's even better, is that He has given me that access through His Word and His Son, Jesus Christ. And the only 2 things required of me are repentance and belief. (Mark 1:15)

Put it Together Using the Tide Technique

¹ SHOUT joyfully to the Lord, all the earth!
² SERVE the Lord with gladness. Come before His courts with joyous SONGS.
³ KNOW that the Lord is God. It is He Who has MADE us, and not we ourselves. We are His PEOPLE, the sheep of His PASTURE.
⁴ Enter His gates with THANKSGIVING, and into His courts with PRAISE. Give THANKS to Him and BLESS His Name.
⁵ For the Lord is GOOD. His MERCY is eternal, and His FAITHFULNESS is from generation to generation

Heaven
Philippians 4:4-9

Memo Devo 2.0
Philippians 4:4-9
Subject: Heaven

Day 1
Phil4:4-5

4 REJOICE in the Lord always. I say again, REJOICE!
5 Let your GENTLENESS be known to all. The Lord is NEAR.

Because this passage starts with two short verses, I lump them together in order to fit the whole thing into one week.

If you've just completed the Memo Devo on Psalm 100 (Worship), then hey, we pick up right where we left off! In fact, these two verses not only continue the encouragement toward worship, they contain a simple prescription for how I should approach every single moment of my life and why. What more could I possibly need!? Well, ahem, plenty, but that's another Memo Devo...or two...or...anyway...

I also think this passage is talking about much more than just how I am to act and think while here on earth. I believe Paul is giving me an actual glimpse into heaven itself. The giveaway to me is his mention of the 'peace' of God, not once (v7), but twice (v9). What are the two things I experience when I trust Jesus as my Savior? The first is Peace with God in heaven (Romans 5:1) and the second is peace with the world, as Jesus has overcome it (Luke 2:14, John 14:27, Philippians 4:7). So, a passage like this gives me not only an example of how I am to approach each day right now, but also of the timeless eternal heavenly bliss to come.

And interestingly, the best place on earth to witness Philippians 4:4-9 in action on daily basis...is around children. (Mark 10:15)

Memo Devo 2.0
Philippians 4:4-9
Subject: Heaven

Day 2
Phil4:6

6 Be ANXIOUS about nothing. But in all THINGS, let your requests be made known to God in prayer and supplication, with THANKSGIVING.

Prayer is an act of worship, even in the expression of need. It is coming before the Throne, praising and petitioning God with bold humility and thanksgiving, to align my will with His until we are one. (John 17:21)

I'm brought back once again to the "backbone" of the New Testament, a text Paul obviously spent a LOT of time pondering, The Sermon on the Mount. Here, I believe he's referencing Matthew 6:25-34 (one could plausibly conclude that they were both circulating the churches at about the same time – in the 50s and/or 60s). In any case, I can't tell you how helpful it's been to me as I wrestle with the truths of God, to deeply ponder Jesus' words in Matthew 5-7 by memorizing and speaking them back. I so encourage you to do the same. They confirm old ideas. They reveal new insights. But mainly they just draw me closer to God.

There's no better way to interpret the words of Jesus' Spirit than by the words of Jesus' mouth. (Galatians 4:6)

Put it Together Using the Tide Technique

4 REJOICE in the Lord always. I say again, REJOICE!
5 Let your GENTLENESS be known to all. The Lord is NEAR.
6 Be ANXIOUS about nothing. But in all THINGS, let your requests be made known to God in prayer and supplication, with THANKSGIVING.

Memo Devo 2.0
Philippians 4:4-9
Subject: Heaven

Day 3
Phil4:7

7 And the PEACE of God—which surpasses all understanding—shall GUARD your hearts and minds in Christ Jesus.

This verse has been the subject of thousands of sermons, greeting cards, and yes, even a kids' song (the true test of fame). And when I ponder it in the context of the previous three verses, I begin to see that the real peace of God doesn't come from Him blessing me, but from me blessing Him.

I tend to put God's peace in a very small box. I praise Him for my new job or my mortgage payment. I say "God is good" when my marriage is healed or my mom's health returns. But what about when 10,000 innocent Sudanese are killed in a civil war? Or a friend dies unexpectedly, leaving a family behind?

God's PEACE – the kind that passes all understanding, the kind that unlocks the gates of heaven – comes from my worshiping Him for Who He Is and what He has done for me on the Cross. It's peace that lies not in earthly outcomes. It is heavenly peace. It is in Christ Jesus. (1Corinthians 13:10)

Put it Together Using the Tide Technique

4 REJOICE in the Lord always. I say again, REJOICE!
5 Let your GENTLENESS be known to all. The Lord is NEAR.
6 Be ANXIOUS about nothing. But in all THINGS, let your requests be made known to God in prayer and supplication, with THANKSGIVING.
7 And the PEACE of God—which surpasses all understanding—shall GUARD your hearts and minds in Christ Jesus.

Memo Devo 2.0
Philippians 4:4-9
Subject: Heaven

Day 4
Phil4:8

8 Finally, brothers, whatever things are TRUE, whatever things are NOBLE, whatever things are RIGHT, whatever things are PURE, whatever things are LOVELY, whatever things are ADMIRABLE, if there is any EXCELLENCE or if there is any PRAISE, think on these things.

Steve's Mnemonic: "TuRNiP LEAP"
True, Right, Noble, Pure, Lovely, Excellent, Admirable, Praiseworthy

Just when you thought Memo Devo 2.0 wasn't as silly as MD1.... Seriously though, this verse is the center of the whole passage for me, and why I think of it as a glimpse into heaven. As an adult, all of these keywords are much more elusive to me than I'd like. But what about when I was a child? Sure, I had my moments of disobedience and discipline, but think about the heart that these words describe. It is a heart that is open, humble, and often vulnerable. It is a heart without prejudice or hatred, at least not instinctively. It is the heart of an eternal optimist, who always assumes the best, and has an unbelievable capacity to love unconditionally.

It is the heart of a child. And of such is God's kingdom (Matt18:1-5).

Put it Together Using the Tide Technique

... 6 Be ANXIOUS about nothing. But in all THINGS, let your requests be made known to God in prayer and supplication, with THANKSGIVING.
7 And the PEACE of God—which surpasses all understanding—shall GUARD your hearts and minds in Christ Jesus.
8 Finally, brothers, whatever things are TRUE, whatever things are NOBLE, whatever things are RIGHT, whatever things are PURE, whatever things are LOVELY, whatever things are ADMIRABLE, if there is any EXCELLENCE or if there is any PRAISE, think on these things.

Memo Devo 2.0
Philippians 4:4-9
Subject: Heaven

Day 5
Phil4:9

9 And that which you have LEARNED and RECEIVED, and have HEARD and UNDERSTOOD in me, DO. And the God of PEACE shall be with you.

Steve's Mnemonic: "HURL" – Heard, Understood, Received, Learned

You know, once the silly spigot has been turned on, it's hard to shut it off. But this mnemonic IS exactly what it needs to be in order for me to remember this very important follow up step to the previous verse. Not only is it just weird enough to be memorable, but it also reminds me that it's not enough to simply seek after a childlike heart and mind. I also need to put them into practice, or HURL them out there into the world in a conspicuous way; not as some kind of spiritual "checklist", but as an act of worship.

Put it Together Using the Tide Technique

4 REJOICE in the Lord always. I say again, REJOICE!
5 Let your GENTLENESS be known to all. The Lord is NEAR.
6 Be ANXIOUS about nothing. But in all THINGS, let your requests be made known to God in prayer and supplication, with THANKSGIVING.
7 And the PEACE of God—which surpasses all understanding—shall GUARD your hearts and minds in Christ Jesus.
8 Finally, brothers, whatever things are TRUE, whatever things are NOBLE, whatever things are RIGHT, whatever things are PURE, whatever things are LOVELY, whatever things are ADMIRABLE, if there is any EXCELLENCE or if there is any PRAISE, think on these things.
9 And that which you have LEARNED and RECEIVED, and have HEARD and UNDERSTOOD in me, DO. And the God of PEACE shall be with you.

My Body
1Corinthians 6:15-20

Memo Devo 2.0
1Corinthians 6:15-20
Subject: My Body

Day 1
1Cor6:15

15 Do you not know that your bodies are the MEMBERS of Christ? Shall I then take the MEMBERS of Christ and make them the MEMBERS of a PROSTITUTE? Absolutely not!

Point to Ponder

The Greek word for 'prostitute' is 'porne'. Given that fact, the full application definitely seems broader than just traditional physical acts of adultery or promiscuity. Paul (i.e. Jesus) is also talking about thoughts, just as Jesus Himself did in Matthew 5:27-30. We will see this confirmed much further as we ponder this whole passage.

Put it Together Using the Tide Technique

I usually start at the end and "tide" back to the beginning. However sometimes I do employ a reverse "rip tide" technique too. Do whichever seems to work best for you. Repeat one phrase at a time, about 10 times or so, adding cumulatively as you go until you can say each cumulative section without looking a couple of times through. Go slowly. Use keywords and mnemonics as triggers to help group words into "chunks".

For example: In this case, it is helpful for me to anchor to the word "members" because it appears three times. Anything I can do to "shrink" the amount of words my brain needs to organize in this first short-term memory stage is a helpful mnemonic. Just knowing I need to say that word three times does that a bit. Economize energy wherever you can. Encourage yourself!

Memo Devo 2.0
1Corinthians 6:15-20
Subject: My Body

Day 2
1Cor6:16-17

16 Do you not know that he who couples himself with a prostitute is one BODY? For two, says He, shall be one FLESH.
17 But the one who is JOINED to the Lord, is one SPIRIT.

Two verses today since they complete a single thought (and really, what's 11 more words between friends, right?). Paul references Genesis 2_24 to point out the seriousness of the problem, as well as its only real solution. Adultery, promiscuity and pornography are bad ideas primarily because they are offenses against God's original design. I am integrating my own flesh with someone or something other than my God-given mate or "ezer neged" in the Hebrew of Geneses 2:18 (whether I have met her yet or not!).

The only way I can overcome this attack on my flesh is by becoming one with Jesus' Spirit. He is the only One powerful enough to enable me to succeed. My own power is insufficient, just as Eve's was not enough in the Garden. And make no mistake, it is the EXACT same enemy. Always. He just uses a different lie, created "juuuust for me". (Let's see how many under 50 actually get that reference.)

Put it Together Using the Tide Technique

15 Do you not know that your bodies are the MEMBERS of Christ? Shall I then take the MEMBERS of Christ and make them the MEMBERS of a PROSTITUTE? Absolutely not!
16 Do you not know that he who couples himself with a prostitute is one BODY? For two, says He, shall be one FLESH.
17 But the one who is JOINED to the Lord, is one SPIRIT.

Memo Devo 2.0
1Corinthians 6:15-20
Subject: My Body

Day 3
1Cor6:18

18 FLEE fornication. Every sin that a man does is OUTSIDE the body. But the one who commits fornication, sins against his OWN body.

"No REALLY," Jesus seems to be saying, "You are not able to handle this. I know sometimes I say things like 'stand firm' and 'be strong', and I do mean it in those cases. But this time let Me be perfectly clear: When faced with sexual sin, you are to FLEE RIGHT INTO MY ARMS. Got it?"

Why? Because sexual sin comes from within me, which is quite literally where Jesus lives. That's why He says sin from within is what truly defiles me (Mark 7:15). It's basically the same thing as what He did to the money changers in the Temple. There was really nothing else for it but complete and, if necessary, violent action. It's ultimately an act of love for His Father, the preservation of His dwelling place.

Put it Together Using the Tide Technique

15 Do you not know that your bodies are the MEMBERS of Christ? Shall I then take the MEMBERS of Christ and make them the MEMBERS of a PROSTITUTE? Absolutely not!
16 Do you not know that he who couples himself with a prostitute is one BODY? For two, says He, shall be one FLESH.
17 But the one who is JOINED to the Lord, is one SPIRIT.
18 FLEE fornication. Every sin that a man does is OUTSIDE the body. But the one who commits fornication, sins against his OWN body.

Memo Devo 2.0
1Corinthians 6:15-20
Subject: My Body

Day 4
1Cor6:19

19 Do you not know that your body is the TEMPLE of the Holy Ghost, Who is IN you; Whom you HAVE from God? And you are not your OWN.

I probably should have lumped this verse in with yesterday's since it's really a repetition of the same truth. Oh well, consider it a free day to catch up! This verse re-states my responsibility as caretaker of God's holy dwelling place within me so clearly and poetically. Sins against my own body go beyond just tainting the physical bond between my God-ordained spouse and me, they affect my spiritual bond with Jesus. It's why David says "Against You, against You only have I sinned..." in Psalm 51:4 after his transgression with Bathsheba.

There is no more important relationship.

Put it Together Using the Tide Technique

15 Do you not know that your bodies are the MEMBERS of Christ? Shall I then take the MEMBERS of Christ and make them the MEMBERS of a PROSTITUTE? Absolutely not!
16 Do you not know that he who couples himself with a prostitute is one BODY? For two, says He, shall be one FLESH.
17 But the one who is JOINED to the Lord, is one SPIRIT.
18 FLEE fornication. Every sin that a man does is OUTSIDE the body. But the one who commits fornication, sins against his OWN body.
19 Do you not know that your body is the TEMPLE of the Holy Ghost, Who is IN you; Whom you HAVE from God? And you are not your OWN.

Memo Devo 2.0
1Corinthians 6:15-20
Subject: My Body

Day 5
1Cor6:20

20 For you are bought for a PRICE. Therefore, GLORIFY God in your BODY and in your SPIRIT. For they are God's.

Ownership. It's important to understand that the value of my life is zero if it remains in my own possession. I am doomed to eternal separation from God.

But when Jesus shed His blood on that Cross, He literally took ownership of my body and my spirit. He redeemed them for real value; for what Paul calls "surpassing value" in Philippians 3:7-8. He made me once again good, perfect, heavenly.

Put it Together Using the Tide Technique

15 Do you not know that your bodies are the MEMBERS of Christ? Shall I then take the MEMBERS of Christ and make them the MEMBERS of a PROSTITUTE? Absolutely not!
16 Do you not know that he who couples himself with a prostitute is one BODY? For two, says He, shall be one FLESH.
17 But the one who is JOINED to the Lord, is one SPIRIT.
18 FLEE fornication. Every sin that a man does is OUTSIDE the body. But the one who commits fornication, sins against his OWN body.
19 Do you not know that your body is the TEMPLE of the Holy Ghost, Who is IN you; Whom you HAVE from God? And you are not your OWN.
20 For you are bought for a PRICE. Therefore, GLORIFY God in your BODY and in your SPIRIT. For they are God's.

Itching Ears
Romans 5:12-17

Memo Devo 2.0
Romans 5:12-17
Subject: Itching Ears

DAY 1
Rom5:12

12 Therefore, just as by ONE man sin entered into the world, and DEATH by sin, so also death spread to ALL men. For all men have SINNED.

Steve's Mnemonic: "DOA"

While the letters aren't exactly in the right order, they do represent the three main keywords in this verse, as well as its main idea: that ever since Adam first sinned, I am "DOA" in this world.

Points to Ponder

This passage points out the problem with Christians believing in the evolutionary hypothesis that living things were living and dying on the earth millions of years before Adam ever sinned. If that were the case, several MAJOR theological problems arise, not the least of which is that the 4th Commandment no longer makes any sense. But the biggest problem by far is that doing so removes sin as the cause of death and renders Christ's atonement for it meaningless.
But here's another very striking thing about this passage. It's as if Paul saw Day-Age Theory coming. It's similar to how John seems to anticipate the question of Jesus' deity from Mormons and others when he clearly declares it 5 times in the first 18 verses of his Gospel. Paul specifically links sin to death *five* times in just these 6 verses alone. And that's *actual* death, not spiritual death. Think about it. If Paul did mean spiritual death, wouldn't it make sense for him to mention that rather important extra qualifier at least once out of those five times? But he doesn't. He only says 'death'.

God means what He says and says what He means. My understanding of it is not a pre-requisite for its veracity.

Memo Devo 2.0
Romans 5:12-17
Subject: Itching Ears

DAY 2
Rom5:13

13 For UNTIL the time of the Law, sin WAS in the world. But sin was not taken into ACCOUNT while there was no Law.

An explanation of how God viewed the sin of everyone from Adam to Moses; including Eve, Enoch, Noah, Abraham, Sarah, Isaac, Jacob, Judah, Joseph, Joshua, Rahab, etc. This is recounted in greater detail in Hebrews 11 and Acts 7.

Before the Law came, there was sin and death; but not before Adam came.

Put it Together Using The Tide technique

12 Therefore, just as by ONE man sin entered into the world, and DEATH by sin, so also death spread to ALL men. For all men have SINNED.
13 For UNTIL the time of the Law, sin WAS in the world. But sin was not taken into ACCOUNT while there was no Law.

---

*I find a good rule of thumb during this first short-term memorization stage is 10 repetitions. Then it's really best to go ahead and recite each verse each day for someone else. I like to involve my kids. But if I can't do that, a fun way to check if something is getting into my long-term memory is to speak the verse back out loud to myself while juggling or folding laundry or doing some other simple task that creates a mild distraction for my brain. Some days are tougher than others, but I try VERY HARD to stay on schedule. I will give myself an extra day to repeat the same devo if things come up or I just don't feel ready to move on.

Memo Devo 2.0
Romans 5:12-17
Subject: Itching Ears

DAY 3
Rom5:14

14 But DEATH reigned from ADAM to MOSES, even over those who did not sin in a similar way to the transgression of Adam (who was the same as Him Who was to come).

Steve's Mnemonic: "DAM" ("Death from Adam to Moses")

Sin became the "dam" of separation between God and me. The only Way back to God is by overcoming death through the forgiveness of my sin. That's the reason Jesus came to earth; to reconcile my relationship with God (Mark 2:10). If I don't link death to Adam's sin, but rather just kind of casually accept that death was already there billions of years earlier, then what I'm saying is that there is no dam of separation, no death, due to sin. And if that's the case, then why do I need Jesus?

But even if Paul's linking of Adam's sin with death for the third time in this passage still isn't enough for me, I can always just take God's word for it:

"For on the day you shall eat thereof, you shall die the death."
- Genesis 2:17

Put it Together Using The Tide Technique

12 Therefore, just as by ONE man sin entered into the world, and DEATH by sin, so also death spread to ALL men. For all men have SINNED.
13 For UNTIL the time of the Law, sin WAS in the world. But sin was not taken into ACCOUNT while there was no Law.
14 But DEATH reigned from ADAM to MOSES, even over those who did not sin in a similar way to the transgression of Adam (who was the same as Him Who was to come).

Memo Devo 2.0
Romans 5:12-17
Subject: Itching Ears

DAY 4
Rom5:15

15 But still, the GIFT is not like the OFFENSE. For if, through the offense of one, many DIED, much MORE so has the GRACE of God and the GIFT (by grace) of the one man, JESUS Christ, ABOUNDED to many.

Steve's Mnemonic: "GO for More"

A rather awkward sentence structure in any translation, but a pretty clear message when broken down logically. The main keywords here are 'gift' and 'offense', as they are the two things being compared. So "GO" makes sense for the first part of a mnemonic. Then the other main point Paul is making is the fact that the grace of Jesus is MORE than the offense of Adam.

This is also the fourth time in these six verses that Paul clearly links our death directly to our sin; this time in an effort to compare and contrast death's poetically powerful remedy, Jesus.

Put it Together Using The Tide Technique

12 Therefore, just as by ONE man sin entered into the world, and DEATH by sin, so also death spread to ALL men. For all men have SINNED.
13 For UNTIL the time of the Law, sin WAS in the world. But sin was not taken into ACCOUNT while there was no Law.
14 But DEATH reigned from ADAM to MOSES, even over those who did not sin in a similar way to the transgression of Adam (who was the same as Him Who was to come).
15 But still, the GIFT is not like the OFFENSE. For if, through the offense of one, many DIED, much MORE so has the GRACE of God and the GIFT (by grace) of the one man, JESUS Christ, ABOUNDED to many.

Memo Devo 2.0
Romans 5:12-17
Subject: Itching Ears

DAY 5
Rom5:16

16 Nor is the GIFT as if it were from one who sinned. Indeed, JUDGMENT unto CONDEMNATION came from one. But the gift unto JUSTIFICATION came from many offenses.

Although, in my opinion, this cannot be cited as another overt statement about sin equaling death in so many words, it is a brilliantly simple re-stating of verse 15, with emphasis on the result of Christ's perfect grace in response to our sin (and death).

Put it Together Using The Tide Technique

12 Therefore, just as by ONE man sin entered into the world, and DEATH by sin, so also death spread to ALL men. For all men have SINNED.
13 For UNTIL the time of the Law, sin WAS in the world. But sin was not taken into ACCOUNT while there was no Law.
14 But DEATH reigned from ADAM to MOSES, even over those who did not sin in a similar way to the transgression of Adam (who was the same as Him Who was to come).
15 But still, the GIFT is not like the OFFENSE. For if, through the offense of one, many DIED, much MORE so has the GRACE of God and the GIFT (by grace) of the one man, JESUS Christ, ABOUNDED to many.
16 Nor is the GIFT as if it were from one who sinned. Indeed, JUDGMENT unto CONDEMNATION came from one. But the gift unto JUSTIFICATION came from many offenses.

Memo Devo 2.0
Romans 5:12-17
Subject: Itching Ears

DAY 6
Rom5:17

17 For if, by the OFFENSE of one, DEATH reigned through one, much MORE so shall those who receive the ABUNDANCE of grace, and the GIFT of righteousness, reign in LIFE through One—Jesus Christ.

I have to confess this last verse is a bear for me. It's so convoluted grammatically, I have a hard time even picking out keywords, much less a plausible mnemonic. If you come up with one, please let me know! But it is definitely another re-statement of verse 15, including a fifth direct equation of sin with death. And it also has one little added bonus. It tells me the result of God's grace in response to my sin and death...NEW LIFE!

Put it Together Using The Tide Technique

12 Therefore, just as by ONE person sin entered into the world, and DEATH by sin, likewise death overcame ALL people, because ALL have sinned.
13 For BEFORE the Law, sin WAS in the world. But sin was not taken into ACCOUNT while there was no Law.
14 But DEATH reigned from ADAM to MOSES, EVEN over those who didn't commit sins SIMILAR to those of Adam, who was the SAME as Him that was to come.
15 But yet the GIFT is not like the OFFENSE. For if through the offense of one, many DIED, much MORE so did the GRACE of God and the GIFT by grace of one man JESUS Christ, ABOUND to many.
16 Indeed, the GIFT is not as if it were from one who sinned. For the CONDEMNATION of many came from one sin. But the JUSTIFICATION of many came from one gracious gift.
17 For if, by the OFFENSE of one, DEATH reigned through one, much MORE so shall those who receive the ABUNDANCE of grace, and the GIFT of righteousness, reign in LIFE through One—Jesus Christ.

Death
2Corinthians 5:1-7

Memo Devo 2.0
2Corinthians 5:1-7
Subject: Death

Day 1
2Cor5:1

1 For we know that if our EARTHLY HOUSE of this tabernacle is destroyed, WE HAVE a building given by God; that is, a HOUSE, made not with HANDS, but ETERNAL, in the HEAVENS.

Steve's Mnemonic: "The 'H's - EH, WH, HH, EH"

I realize mnemonics like this are largely only beneficial to warped brains like mine. But remember, as far as I'm concerned, the best memory aids are those that organize my thoughts in an interesting way so that the verse is a bit more manageable during the short-term memorization stage. If you feel you can fare better with a different memory trigger or even no trigger at all, there are no wrong helps, only wrong answers.

Point to Ponder

Whatever date I ascribe to each of the Gospels, Paul is clearly mirroring John 2:19-22, Mark 14:58 and Matthew 26:61 here. Whether it is a mansion made of pearls on a golden street in the clouds, or simply a blissful "permanent present" with The Great I Am, it's the most peaceful place I can never imagine.

Memo Devo 2.0
2Corinthians 5:1-7
Subject: Death

Day 2
2Cor5:2-3

2 For therefore we SIGH, desiring to be clothed with our house, which is from Heaven.
3 Because if we are CLOTHED, we shall not be found NAKED.

The reference in v3 is convenient because it points to Genesis 3, making it a good candidate for a mnemonic. I call this "verse symmetry". It occurs when two or more verses referencing a similar number have complementary meanings. It's usually more direct than it is here, comparing verses to verses, but this still works for me. My being clothed in Jesus' Spirit now relates numerically as well as figuratively to Adam and Eve's literal need for clothing in the Garden.

Put it Together Using The Tide Technique

1 For we know that if our EARTHLY HOUSE of this tabernacle is destroyed, WE HAVE a building given by God; that is, a HOUSE, made not with HANDS, but ETERNAL, in the HEAVENS.
2 For therefore we SIGH, desiring to be clothed with our house, which is from Heaven.
3 Because if we are CLOTHED, we shall not be found NAKED.

Memo Devo 2.0
2Corinthians 5:1-7
Subject: Death

Day 3
2Cor5:2-3

4 For INDEED, we who are in this tabernacle sigh and are BURDENED, because we do not wish to be UNCLOTHED but clothed; so that MORTALITY might be swallowed up in LIFE.

What a great statement of what is meant by the term "life". So often I miss this. It's not poverty that's swallowed up by life. It's not sickness, or pain, or suffering. It's death. The only permanent separation from the Father. To me that means the "life that is truly life" and the "life to the full" are not found in this life, but in the next. This is what makes it possible for me to pray in all circumstances. This is why God is still love to me, even in the face of overwhelming despair. In the end, there is life for all who believe (John 1:12).

And here's the real mind-boggling part: No matter who that may exclude, there will be no more tears on that Day; only joy. (Revelation 21:4)

Put it Together Using The Tide Technique

1 For we know that if our EARTHLY HOUSE of this tabernacle is destroyed, WE HAVE a building given by God; that is, a HOUSE, made not with HANDS, but ETERNAL, in the HEAVENS.
2 For therefore we SIGH, desiring to be clothed with our house, which is from Heaven.
3 Because if we are CLOTHED, we shall not be found NAKED.
4 For INDEED, we who are in this tabernacle sigh and are BURDENED, because we do not wish to be UNCLOTHED but clothed; so that MORTALITY might be swallowed up in LIFE.

Memo Devo 2.0
2Corinthians 5:1-7
Subject: Death

Day 4
2Cor5:5

5 And He Who has created us for this thing, is God; Who also has given to us the EARNEST PORTION of the Spirit.

What is going on in this life is what the Bible often refers to as "firstfruits". It is but a glimpse of the things to come; a small sample of a heavenly glory so intense that we cannot possibly comprehend it. And that too is by design (Hebrews 11:6). Yet God, in His amazing love, has revealed just enough to those with whom He is pleased in order to accomplish His purposes in time (Hebrews 10:24). This is at once dumbfounding and amazingly comforting.

Put it Together Using The Tide Technique

1 For we know that if our EARTHLY HOUSE of this tabernacle is destroyed, WE HAVE a building given by God; that is, a HOUSE, made not with HANDS, but ETERNAL, in the HEAVENS.
2 For therefore we SIGH, desiring to be clothed with our house, which is from Heaven.
3 Because if we are CLOTHED, we shall not be found NAKED.
4 For INDEED, we who are in this tabernacle sigh and are BURDENED, because we do not wish to be UNCLOTHED but clothed; so that MORTALITY might be swallowed up in LIFE.
5 And He Who has created us for this thing, is God; Who also has given to us the EARNEST PORTION of the Spirit.

Memo Devo 2.0
2Corinthians 5:1-7
Subject: Death

Day 5
2Cor5:6-7

6 Therefore we are always BOLD; though we know that while we are at HOME in the body, we are ABSENT from the Lord.
7 For we walk by faith, and not by sight.

Verse 6 is one I often quote in the face of death. It is a great comfort to those of us who truly believe. Verse 7 is also famous, but I usually quote that one in more of a temporal context, having to do with worldly provision or protection. Why?
To be sure, Jesus provides peace in all circumstances, having overcome the world by His precious blood. But it seems to me the most powerful context of verse 7 is the same as that of verse 6. It is an eternal context. (Matthew 6:19-21, Mark 4:2-19)

Put it Together Using The Tide Technique

1 For we know that if our EARTHLY HOUSE of this tabernacle is destroyed, WE HAVE a building given by God; that is, a HOUSE, made not with HANDS, but ETERNAL, in the HEAVENS.
2 For therefore we SIGH, desiring to be clothed with our house, which is from Heaven.
3 Because if we are CLOTHED, we shall not be found NAKED.
4 For INDEED, we who are in this tabernacle sigh and are BURDENED, because we do not wish to be UNCLOTHED but clothed; so that MORTALITY might be swallowed up in LIFE.
5 And He Who has created us for this thing, is God; Who also has given to us the EARNEST PORTION of the Spirit.
6 Therefore we are always BOLD; though we know that while we are at HOME in the body, we are ABSENT from the Lord.
7 For we walk by faith, and not by sight.

Marriage
Genesis 2:18-25

Memo Devo 2.0
Genesis 2:18-25
Subject: Marriage

DAY 1
Gen2:18

18 And the Lord God said, "It is not good that ADAM should be alone. I will make a PERFECT MATE for him."

Jesus' Spirit is my best instructor (2Timothy 3:16, John 17:17). It's so refreshing to ponder the poetry of God's human creation. It's the ultimate beauty, regardless of one's politics.

Most mainstream versions of the Bible use the word "man" in this verse, instead of the Hebrew text, ADAM, which means only "human being". Later in this passage, we'll see that Adam was indeed clearly created as a man, but since there are different Hebrew words for "masculine human" in places like Genesis 1:27, 2:23-24, Exodus 13:12, Deuteronomy 4:16 and elsewhere, ADAM seems a better representation of the intended meaning here.

The other Hebrew keyword, which I am translating as PERFECT MATE, is the two-word phrase "ezer neged", which literally means "fitted aid" or "aid, as in a counterpart or opposite part". Regardless, the most important thing to remember at this point about these two keywords (or creations) is that they are complementary in every way; a perfect match.

Put it Together Using the Tide Technique

Whichever translation I use, the words for ADAM and PERFECT MATE make the best keywords here. As I begin to embed the verse in my short-term memory by way of repetition (at least 10 times), I start at the end and "tide" my way back, cumulatively adding a single phrase at a time, like a tide washing in and out, until I reach the beginning.

Memo Devo 2.0
Genesis 2:18-25
Subject: Marriage

DAY 2
Gen2:19

19 So the Lord God FORMED of the earth every BEAST of the field and every BIRD of the heaven and BROUGHT them to Adam, to see what he would call them. For whatever Adam NAMED the living creature, so was the name thereof.

Notice the opening phrase of this verse, "formed of the earth". It doesn't say God "brought forth from the earth" every creature or "took from the earth". It says, "formed of the earth". In fact, it's the same word that's used in verse 7 for the formation of Adam himself, "yatsar". It's as if God created special "prototypes" of each animal all over again especially for Adam, right there out of the Garden dirt, just because...well, that's how He rolls.

Put it Together Using the Tide Technique*

18 And the Lord God said, "It is not good that ADAM should be alone. I will make a PERFECT MATE for him."
19 So the Lord God FORMED of the earth every BEAST of the field and every BIRD of the heaven and BROUGHT them to Adam, to see what he would call them. For whatever Adam NAMED the living creature, so was the name thereof.

*Some folks, (including my own Mom) prefer using a "riptide" or reverse tide technique a lot of the time. No problem at all. Just start at the beginning of v19 and cumulatively ADD one phrase at a time, tiding FORWARD, until you can comfortably say v19 without the text. Then go back and employ the regular tide technique to add v18. And remember to speak it back to someone once you have it!

Memo Devo 2.0
Genesis 2:18-25
Subject: Marriage

DAY 3
Gen2:20

20 Therefore, Adam gave names to all CATTLE, and to the BIRDS of the heaven, and to every BEAST of the field. But he did not FIND a perfect mate for himself.

The distinction between "cattle" and "beasts of the field" is simply "domesticated" (cows, goats, sheep, oxen, etc.) as opposed to "wild" (monkeys, elephants, lions, etc.). Interestingly though, no "cattle" are mentioned in the previous verse, when God is forming all these animals (again). Could it be that Adam made the decisions on which "beasts" would become "cattle" at that same time?

Put it Together Using the Tide Technique*

18 And the Lord God said, "It is not good that ADAM should be alone. I will make a PERFECT MATE for him."
19 So the Lord God FORMED of the earth every BEAST of the field and every BIRD of the heaven and BROUGHT them to Adam, to see what he would call them. For whatever Adam NAMED the living creature, so was the name thereof.
20 Therefore, Adam gave names to all CATTLE, and to the BIRDS of the heaven, and to every BEAST of the field. But he did not FIND a perfect mate for himself.

*Start at the end and "tide" back to the beginning, one phrase at a time, adding cumulatively as you go. Go slowly, using the CAPITALIZED keywords and mnemonics as triggers to help group words into "chunks". More at 5talentsaudio.com/tide.

Memo Devo 2.0
Genesis 2_18-25
Subject: Marriage

DAY 4
Gen2_21

21 Therefore, the Lord God caused a heavy SLEEP to fall upon Adam, and he slept. And He took one of his RIBS and closed up the flesh in its place.

The first surgery! And God is both surgeon and anesthetist. But I think He can multitask it, don't you? Seriously though, think of it. God has just finished RE-forming every creature from nothing right in front of Adam, just so he can name them all. And yet, only after Adam decides *he* is still not satisfied with the results, does God make yet another (and, I would argue, His most beautiful) creation. And even then, He doesn't do it in a beautiful (or at the very least elegant) kind of way. He is really quite messy about it. It reminds me of when Jesus healed the blind men in John 9 and Mark 8 by spitting and making mud to put over their eyes.

Put it Together Using the Tide Technique

18 And the Lord God said, "It is not good that ADAM should be alone. I will make a PERFECT MATE for him."
19 So the Lord God FORMED of the earth every BEAST of the field and every BIRD of the heaven and BROUGHT them to Adam, to see what he would call them. For whatever Adam NAMED the living creature, so was the name thereof.
20 Therefore, Adam GAVE names to all CATTLE, and to the BIRDS of the heaven, and to every BEAST of the field. But he did not FIND a perfect mate for himself.
21 Therefore, the Lord God caused a heavy SLEEP to fall upon Adam, and he slept. And He took one of his RIBS and closed up the flesh in its place.

Memo Devo 2.0
Genesis 2:18-25
Subject: Marriage

DAY 5
Gen 2:22

22 And with the RIB which the Lord God had taken from Adam, He made a WOMAN, and BROUGHT her to him.

God is continually serving Adam, but in His own way, not necessarily the easiest way. Of course, He could have made the woman any way He wanted to, without involving Adam at all. But notice, His amazing act of creativity not only results in Eve literally coming from "one flesh" with Adam, but it also involves putting His child to sleep; one of the most intimate and tender acts any of us parents can ever experience. In fact, though it doesn't say so in Scripture, I like to imagine that God paused right then just so He could watch His beloved boy sleep the sleep of the innocent for just a few seconds before blessing him with what He knew would be his greatest treasure in this world – his perfect mate!

Put it Together Using the Tide Technique

18 And the Lord God said, "It is not good that ADAM should be alone. I will make a PERFECT MATE for him."
19 So the Lord God FORMED of the earth every BEAST of the field and every BIRD of the heaven and BROUGHT them to Adam, to see what he would call them. For whatever Adam NAMED the living creature, so was the name thereof.
20 Therefore, Adam GAVE names to all CATTLE, and to the BIRDS of the heaven, and to every BEAST of the field. But he did not FIND a perfect mate for himself.
21 Therefore, the Lord God caused a heavy SLEEP to fall upon Adam, and he slept. And He took one of his RIBS and closed up the flesh in its place.
22 And with the RIB which the Lord God had taken from Adam, He made a WOMAN, and BROUGHT her to him.

Memo Devo 2.0
Genesis 2:18-25
Subject: Marriage

DAY 6
Gen2:23

23 Then Adam said, "This, now, is BONE of my bones, and FLESH of my FLESH. She shall be called 'woman', because she was taken out of the man."

Steve's Mnemonic: BFF

For the first time, the Hebrew uses two gender specific words for both man "iysh" and woman "ishshah". They are perfectly fitted for each other, created from the same one flesh and intended to return to that same one flesh as husband and wife.

Put it Together Using the Tide Technique

...19 So the Lord God FORMED of the earth every BEAST of the field and every BIRD of the heaven and BROUGHT them to Adam, to see what he would call them. For whatever Adam NAMED the living creature, so was the name thereof.
20 Therefore, Adam GAVE names to all CATTLE, and to the BIRDS of the heaven, and to every BEAST of the field. But he did not FIND a perfect mate for himself.
21 Therefore, the Lord God caused a heavy SLEEP to fall upon Adam, and he slept. And He took one of his RIBS and closed up the flesh in its place.
22 And with the rib which the Lord God had taken from Adam, He made a WOMAN, and brought her to him.
23 Then Adam said, "This, now, is BONE of my bones, and FLESH of my flesh. She shall be called 'woman', because she was taken out of the man."

Memo Devo 2.0
Genesis 2:18-25
Subject: Marriage

DAY 7
Gen2:24

24 THEREFORE, man shall LEAVE his father and his mother, and shall CLING to his wife. And they shall be one flesh.

Steve's Mnemonic: TLC

It's almost as if God should have added the word "again" at the end of this verse to make sure we got it. But He does repeat basically the same thing He said in the previous verse which, in a biblical sense, is kinda the same as shouting it or saayyying it reeaally slooowwwlyy sooo I doonnn'ttt mmmmissssss it:

"Hey, don't miss this! I formed you as a man and a woman from the same physical flesh! When you come together now, you return to that same physical flesh! It is a BIG DEAL!" (1Corinthians 6:16)

Put it Together Using the Tide Technique

...20 Therefore, Adam GAVE names to all CATTLE, and to the BIRDS of the heaven, and to every BEAST of the field. But he did not FIND a perfect mate for himself.
21 Therefore, the Lord God caused a heavy SLEEP to fall upon Adam, and he slept. And He took one of his RIBS and closed up the flesh in its place.
22 And with the rib which the Lord God had taken from Adam, He made a WOMAN, and brought her to him.
23 Then Adam said, "This, now, is BONE of my bones, and FLESH of my flesh. She shall be called 'woman', because she was taken out of the man."
24 THEREFORE, man shall LEAVE his father and his mother, and shall CLING to his wife. And they shall be one flesh.

Memo Devo 2.0
Genesis 2:18-25
Subject: Marriage

DAY 8
Gen2:25

25 And they were both NAKED, the man and his wife, and they were NOT ASHAMED.

Before sin enters the world, Adam and his wife are naked, both spiritually and physically. They are sublimely and fearlessly content to put God at the center of their consciousness. Once they put themselves at the center, they become afraid and in need of clothing. (2Corinthians 5:2)

Put it Together Using the Tide Technique

18 And the Lord God said, "It is not good that ADAM should be alone. I will make a PERFECT MATE for him."
19 So the Lord God FORMED from the earth every BEAST of the field and every BIRD of the heaven and BROUGHT them to Adam, to see what he would call them. For whatever Adam NAMED the living creature, so was the name thereof.
20 Adam therefore GAVE names to all CATTLE, and to the BIRDS of the heaven, and to every BEAST of the field. But he did not FIND a perfect mate for himself.
21 Therefore the Lord God caused a heavy SLEEP to fall upon Adam, and he slept. And He took one of his RIBS, and closed up the flesh in its place.
22 And with the rib which the Lord God had taken from Adam, He made a WOMAN, and brought her to him.
23 Then Adam said, "This now is BONE of my bones, and FLESH of my flesh. She shall be called 'woman', because she was taken out of the man."
24 THEREFORE, man shall LEAVE his father and his mother, and shall CLING to his wife, and they shall be one flesh.
25 And they were both NAKED, the man and his wife, and they were NOT ASHAMED.

The Passover
Exodus 12:1-12

Memo Devo 2.0
Exodus12:1-12
Subject: The Passover

Day 1
Ex12:1-2

1 Then the Lord SPOKE to Moses and Aaron in the land of Egypt, saying,
2 "This MONTH shall be to you the BEGINNING OF MONTHS. It shall be to you the FIRST month of the year."

Steve's Mnemonic: "Beginning of months"

This is a "subjective" mnemonic, meaning it is more literal (and less silly). It is an "earnest portion" of the larger subject of these two verses. Again, the idea is to "trigger" my brain to fill in the rest with as few clues as possible.

Points to Ponder

God has not explicitly revealed when Creation Week happened on the calendar. But He has very clearly revealed to us when the calendar year is to begin – at Passover. In fact, He says it in two different ways here in verse 2 and also in Leviticus 23:5.

This is a great passage to learn and speak back at Easter, similar to speaking back Luke 2:1-20 at Christmas. It teaches our children exactly WHO Christ is in the whole redemptive plan of God for ALL of His children.

Memo Devo 2.0
Exodus12_1-12
Subject: The Passover

Day 2
Ex12:3

3 "Speak to all the congregation of Israel, saying, 'On the TENTH of this month, let every man take a LAMB according to the HOUSE of the fathers. A LAMB for a HOUSE.'"

Steve's Mnemonic: "2 + 2 = 10"

2 lambs + 2 houses = 10th of the month. This one is admittedly out there a bit and I don't HAVE to have a mnemonic for every verse. In fact, if I can get along without one, I prefer it. But if I am struggling with a verse, I find they are great personalized aides. Remember, it's not a substitute for the hard work of repetition, just a way to help organize the short-term memorization process.

Put it Together Using The Tide Technique*

1 Then the Lord SPOKE to Moses and Aaron in the land of Egypt, saying,
2 "This MONTH shall be to you the BEGINNING OF MONTHS. It shall be to you the FIRST month of the year.
3 "Speak to all the congregation of Israel, saying, 'On the TENTH of this month, let every man take a LAMB according to the HOUSE of the fathers. A LAMB for a HOUSE.'"

*After having put verse 3 in my short-term memory, rather than going back to verse 1 and trying to run all three verses that I have learned together just yet, I first only go back to verse 2 and begin there, running 2 and 3 until I can do just those two comfortably. Only then do I go back and add verse 1 and try to do the whole thing together, like a tide slowly going in and out over the whole passage until it's solidified in my long-term memory and ready for testing. With this process, I am actually repeating the verses more often than if I were doing a traditional approach of going back to the beginning every time because my brain feels less stressed and is more encouraged by more successful run-throughs of smaller sections. More at 5talentsaudio.com/tide-technique.

Memo Devo 2.0
Exodus 12:1-12
Subject: The Passover

Day 3
Ex 12:4

4 "AND if the HOUSEhold is too LITTLE for the lamb, he shall SHARE with his next door neighbor. ACCORDING to the number of PEOPLE and their EATING shall you make your COUNT for the LAMB."

Steve's Mnemonic: "A LITTLE HOUSE SHAREs A PiECe of LAMB"
Remember, only the CAPS are part of my memory trigger. The lower case letters only serve to make it a coherent sentence. Again, I realize this is pretty wacky. But it works for me and that is all that matters when choosing your mnemonics.

Point to Ponder

The sharing of the lamb with those less fortunate is, of course, a basic Judeo-Christian doctrine. The more I separate myself from others within the church body, the less of God's provision I will experience, both physically and spiritually. Study together. Eat together. Pray together. Slow down together. Live life together. (Matthew 25:29, Acts 2:42-47)

Put it Together Using The Tide Technique

1 Then the Lord SPOKE to Moses and Aaron in the land of Egypt, saying,
2 "This MONTH shall be to you the BEGINNING OF MONTHS. It shall be to you the FIRST month of the year.
3 "Speak to all the congregation of Israel, saying, 'On the TENTH of this month, let every man take a LAMB according to the HOUSE of the fathers. A LAMB for a HOUSE.'
4 "AND if the HOUSEhold is too LITTLE for the lamb, he shall SHARE with his next door neighbor. ACCORDING to the number of PEOPLE and their EATING shall you make your COUNT for the LAMB."

Memo Devo 2.0
Exodus12:1-12
Subject: The Passover

Day 4
Ex12:5

5 "Your lamb shall be without BLEMISH; a male of a year old. You may take it from the lambs or from the KIDS."

Now we see the first direct connection between Passover and Jesus' death and resurrection. Just as the first Passover lamb was perfect by Earth's standards, the last One (Jesus) is perfect by Heaven's. The "Last Supper" is literally the last Passover meal as originally instituted by God. That is why there is no lamb mentioned in the Upper Room. Jesus is the lamb. (John 1:29)

Put it Together Using The Tide Technique*

1 Then the Lord SPOKE to Moses and Aaron in the land of Egypt, saying,
2 "This MONTH shall be to you the BEGINNING OF MONTHS. It shall be to you the FIRST month of the year.
3 "Speak to all the congregation of Israel, saying, 'On the TENTH of this month, let every man take a LAMB according to the HOUSE of the fathers. A LAMB for a HOUSE.'
4 "AND if the HOUSEhold is too LITTLE for the lamb, he shall SHARE with his next door neighbor. ACCORDING to the number of PEOPLE and their EATING shall you make your COUNT for the LAMB.
5 "Your lamb shall be without BLEMISH; a male of a year old. You may take it from the lambs or from the KIDS."

*I try to memorize a maximum of 5 verses each week unless I am including extra verses as part of a single idea. For example, on Day 5 I will include vv1-6 but on Day 6 (Monday) I'll recite only vv3-7. It's good to bite off small sections at a time. Eventually, I'll make my way back to the very beginning again. But for now, I just think in terms of what I'm adding each day and each week. Slow and steady.

Memo Devo 2.0
Exodus 12:1-12
Subject: The Passover

Day 5
Ex12:6

6 "And you shall keep it until the 14TH day of this month. Then ALL the multitude of the congregation of Israel shall kill it at DUSK."

Point to Ponder

Again, the parallels are obvious and powerful, right down to the hour of the lamb's death on Friday. Also notice that ALL the children of Israel are involved in the killing of the lamb. (John 1:12).

ALL the congregation of Israel kills the lamb at dusk on Friday of Passover Week in order to be saved from death. (Mark 15:34-37)

Put it Together Using The Tide Technique

1 Then the Lord SPOKE to Moses and Aaron in the land of Egypt, saying,
2 "This MONTH shall be to you the BEGINNING OF MONTHS. It shall be to you the FIRST month of the year.
3 "Speak to all the congregation of Israel, saying, 'On the TENTH of this month, let every man take a LAMB according to the HOUSE of the fathers. A LAMB for a HOUSE.'
4 "AND if the HOUSEhold is too LITTLE for the lamb, he shall SHARE with his next door neighbor. ACCORDING to the number of PEOPLE and their EATING shall you make your COUNT for the LAMB.
5 "Your lamb shall be without BLEMISH; a male of a year old. You may take it from the lambs or from the KIDS.
6 "And you shall keep it until the 14TH day of this month. Then ALL the multitude of the congregation of Israel shall kill it at DUSK."

Memo Devo 2.0
Exodus 12:1-12
Subject: The Passover

Day 6
Ex12:7

7 "Afterward, they shall take the BLOOD and strike it on the FRAMES of the doorways of the houses where they shall EAT it."

"Take. Eat. This is *my* body...This is *my* blood of that *New Testament*" (Mark 14:22-24, *emphases mine*)

The Disciples had to have perceived the comparison Jesus was making in the Upper Room. The only remaining question now was on what "frames" would the Lamb of God's blood be struck? But one doesn't have to ponder long for that answer either.

It's poetic that God takes the ultimate sign of fear, The Roman Cross, and turns it into the ultimate sign of security. Jesus bore His perfect blood of salvation on that Cross, just like those "perfect" lambs did on those door frames of Goshen 1500 years earlier.

Put it Together Using The Tide Technique

...3 "Speak to all the congregation of Israel, saying, 'On the TENTH of this month, let every man take a LAMB according to the HOUSE of the fathers. A LAMB for a HOUSE.'
4 "AND if the HOUSEhold is too LITTLE for the lamb, he shall SHARE with his next-door neighbor. ACCORDING to the number of PEOPLE and their EATING shall you make your COUNT for the LAMB.
5 "Your lamb shall be without BLEMISH; a male of a year old. You may take it from the lambs or from the KIDS.
6 "And you shall keep it until the 14TH day of this month. Then ALL the multitude of the congregation of Israel shall kill it at DUSK.
7 "Afterward, they shall take the BLOOD and strike it on the FRAMES of the doorways of the houses where they shall EAT it."

Memo Devo 2.0
Exodus12:1-12
Subject: The Passover

Day 7
Ex12:8-10

8 "And they shall eat the FLESH that same NIGHT, roasted with FIRE, and with Unleavened Bread and Sour Herbs.
9 "Do not eat it Raw Or Boiled in water, but roasted with FIRE, including his Head, Feet, and Entrails.
10 "And you shall RESERVE nothing of it to the MORNING. Rather, that which remains of it UNTIL MORNING you shall burn with FIRE."

Steve's Mnemonic: "Tonight's FLESH on FIRE in the BUSHes is ROB's HeFEr (RESERVEd UNTIL MORNING)"

Welcome back to the deepest recesses of my mind! Scary, huh? But if you ponder the CAPS in both the mnemonic and the 3 verses, it makes sense...eventually...at least to me. The goal, as always, is to reduce the long passage down to a single memorable sentence for short-term memorization purposes only. I combine these 3 verses because they are, to me, one thought, and therefore easier to memorize together.

Put it Together Using The Tide Technique

...6 "And you shall keep it until the 14TH day of this month. Then ALL the multitude of the congregation of Israel shall kill it at DUSK.
7 "Afterward, they shall take the BLOOD and strike it on the FRAMES of the doorways of the houses where they shall EAT it.
8 "And they shall eat the FLESH that same NIGHT, roasted with FIRE, and with Unleavened Bread and Sour Herbs.
9 "Do not eat it Raw Or Boiled in water, but roasted with FIRE, including his Head, Feet, and Entrails.
10 "And you shall RESERVE nothing of it to the MORNING. Rather, that which remains of it UNTIL MORNING you shall burn with FIRE."

Memo Devo 2.0
Exodus12:1-12
Subject: The Passover

Day 8
Ex12:11

11 "And you shall eat it like this: with your SHIRTS tucked in, your SHOES on your feet, and your STAFFS in your hands. And you shall eat it quickly. For it is the Lord's Passover."

Steve's Mnemonic: "Shirts, Shoes & Staffs"

Since "girding one's loins" gets an almost universally comic usage in today's culture, it becomes distracting to use the older translation. So, I do what any self-respecting ex-radio guy would do: I make an alliteration and tuck in my SHIRT.

Put it Together Using The Tide Technique*

...7 "Afterward, they shall take the BLOOD and strike it on the FRAMES of the doorways of the houses where they shall EAT it.
8 "And they shall eat the FLESH that same NIGHT, roasted with FIRE, and with Unleavened Bread and Sour Herbs.
9 "Do not eat it Raw Or Boiled in water, but roasted with FIRE, including his Head, Feet, and Entrails.
10 "And you shall RESERVE nothing of it to the MORNING. Rather, that which remains of it UNTIL MORNING you shall burn with FIRE.
11 "And you shall eat it like this: with your SHIRTS tucked in, your SHOES on your feet, and your STAFFS in your hands. And you shall eat it quickly. For it is the Lord's Passover."

*Only tide back 5 verses or so each day during the week in order to keep each day's goal smaller. Everyone is different. Keep your personal number reachable but challenging. The bigger goal of tiding back to this week's first verse and speaking back this week's whole section to someone (vv6-12) comes tomorrow. Then on Friday, I will attempt to speak back the entire passage (vv1-12). Take your time, though. Don't give up if you aren't able to master this one by Friday. There's no deadline. Be still. Pray for the Spirit to speak Truth to you personally through His Word. He will do it.

Memo Devo 2.0
Exodus12:1-12
Subject: The Passover

Day 9
Ex12:12

12 "For I will PASS through the land of Egypt that same night, and will kill all the FIRSTBORN in the land of Egypt, both MAN and BEAST. And I will execute JUDGMENT upon all the gods of Egypt. I am the Lord."

Put it Together Using The Tide Technique*

...6 "And you shall keep it until the 14TH day of this month. Then ALL the multitude of the congregation of Israel shall kill it at DUSK.
7 "Afterward, they shall take the BLOOD and strike it on the FRAMES of the doorways of the houses where they shall EAT it.
8 "And they shall eat the FLESH that same NIGHT, roasted with FIRE, and with Unleavened Bread and Sour Herbs.
9 "Do not eat it Raw Or Boiled in water, but roasted with FIRE, including his Head, Feet, and Entrails.
10 "And you shall RESERVE nothing of it to the MORNING. Rather, that which remains of it UNTIL MORNING you shall burn with FIRE.
11 "And you shall eat it like this: with your SHIRTS tucked in, your SHOES on your feet, and your STAFFS in your hands. And you shall eat it quickly. For it is the Lord's Passover.
12 "For I will PASS through the land of Egypt that same night, and will kill all the FIRSTBORN in the land of Egypt, both MAN and BEAST. And I will execute JUDGMENT upon all the gods of Egypt. I am the Lord."

*Normally, I don't try to speak back more than 5 verses a week, but this would be another exception to that rule.

Memo Devo 2.0
Exodus 12:1-12
Subject: The Passover

Day 10

Put it Together Using The Tide Technique*

1 Then the Lord SPOKE to Moses and Aaron in the land of Egypt, saying,
2 "This MONTH shall be to you the BEGINNING OF MONTHS. It shall be to you the FIRST month of the year.
3 "Speak to all the congregation of Israel, saying, 'On the TENTH of this month, let every man take a LAMB according to the HOUSE of the fathers. A LAMB for a HOUSE.'
4 "AND if the HOUSEhold is too LITTLE for the lamb, he shall SHARE with his next-door neighbor. ACCORDING to the number of PEOPLE and their EATING shall you make your COUNT for the LAMB.
5 "Your lamb shall be without BLEMISH; a male of a year old. You may take it from the lambs or from the KIDS.
6 "And you shall keep it until the 14TH day of this month. Then ALL the multitude of the congregation of Israel shall kill it at DUSK.
7 "Afterward, they shall take the BLOOD and strike it on the FRAMES of the doorways of the houses where they shall EAT it.
8 "And they shall eat the FLESH that same NIGHT, roasted with FIRE, and with Unleavened Bread and Sour Herbs.
9 "Do not eat it Raw Or Boiled in water, but roasted with FIRE, including his Head, Feet, and Entrails.
10 "And you shall RESERVE nothing of it to the MORNING. Rather, that which remains of it UNTIL MORNING you shall burn with FIRE.
11 "And you shall eat it like this: with your SHIRTS tucked in, your SHOES on your feet, and your STAFFS in your hands. And you shall eat it quickly. For it is the Lord's Passover.
12 "For I will PASS through the land of Egypt that same night, and will kill all the FIRSTBORN in the land of Egypt, both MAN and BEAST. And I will execute JUDGMENT upon all the gods of Egypt. I am the Lord."

Love, Part 2
Psalm 51:1-13

Memo Devo 2.0
Psalm 51:1-13
Subject: Love, Part 2

Day 1
Ps51:1-3

1 Have MERCY upon me, O God, according to your LOVING-KINDNESS. According to the MULTITUDE of your compassions, put away my iniquities.
2 WASH me thoroughly from my iniquity and cleanse me from my sin. 3 For I KNOW my iniquities, and my sin is ever BEFORE me.

Points to Ponder

I put these first three verses together because they are all part of the same thought and thereby actually easier for me to remember than taking one verse per day. I can't emphasize enough how every verse should be approached this way, with the LOGIC of it in mind first and foremost. I am never merely collecting and arranging syllables in an attempt to mindlessly regurgitate them and meet some arbitrary prideful goal. Nor should I let my children do so either. This is a process of MEDITATION on Jesus' words in order to lay hold of the deep abiding truths within them. (John 14:15, John 15:7, John 17:17)

I call this passage "Love, Part 2" because it is just as clear an explanation of true love as Paul's is in 1Cor13, with the linchpin being The Beatitudes of Matthew 5. By that I mean the common thread between David's contrition here and Paul's definition there is that without the Father's mercy (i.e Jesus), neither are possible. David's CONTRITION, not just his forgiveness, is dependent on God's love. (James 4:8-10, 1John 4:7-12, 1Corinthians 13:6, Matthew 5:3)

Memo Devo 2.0
Psalm 51:1-13
Subject: Love, Part 2

Day 2
Ps51:4

4 AGAINST You; against You only have I sinned and done evil in Your sight; that You may be JUST when You SPEAK and PURE when You JUDGE.

Steve's Mnemonic: "JaSPer J"

This is one of those weird mnemonics that just works for me. The first line is the famous one, so no special aids required there. Although note the separation of "sinned" (omitted obedience) and "done evil" (committed disobedience); much the same as he uses both "sin" and "iniquity" elsewhere in this passage. It's a useful reminder to me that disobedience comes in both forms.

Then that beautifully simple and elegant statement of God's holiness in the second part points back to Him as not only the Revealer of my sin, but also its Redeemer. Without Him, there is no standard, no Savior, no Truth.

Put it Together Using the Tide Technique

1 Have MERCY upon me, O God, according to your LOVING-KINDNESS. According to the MULTITUDE of your compassions, put away my iniquities.
2 WASH me thoroughly from my iniquity and cleanse me from my sin. 3 For I KNOW my iniquities, and my sin is ever BEFORE me.
4 AGAINST You; against You only have I sinned and done evil in Your sight; that You may be JUST when You SPEAK and PURE when You JUDGE.

Memo Devo 2.0
Psalm 51:1-13
Subject: Love, Part 2

Day 3
Ps51:5-6

5 Behold, I was BORN in iniquity. And in sin has my mother CONCEIVED me.
6 Behold, You love truth to the core. Therefore, You have taught me wisdom in my core.

Steve's Mnemonic: "LIMIT WhiP" "...**L**ove...**I**n **M**y **I**nmost **T**houghts ...**W**isdom.... **H**idden **P**laces."

Welcome back to the deepest, weirdest recesses of my brain! My "inmost thoughts", if you will. But this is exactly how it should be for you too! Mnemonics need to be deeply personal to the point of...well, oddity. Remember the goal in this phase is to help my brain parse the text and then fill in the gaps, resulting in less work, more relaxation and hopefully more success. Once I am comfortable moving from thought to thought, I can then begin the more meditative long-term memorization phase, where great treasures of revelation from the Spirit await! (John 17:17)

Put it Together Using the Tide Technique

1 Have MERCY upon me, O God, according to your LOVING-KINDNESS. According to the MULTITUDE of your compassions, put away my iniquities.
2 WASH me thoroughly from my iniquity and cleanse me from my sin. 3 For I KNOW my iniquities, and my sin is ever BEFORE me.
4 AGAINST You; against You only have I sinned and done evil in Your sight; that You may be JUST when You SPEAK and PURE when You JUDGE.
5 Behold, I was BORN in iniquity. And in sin has my mother CONCEIVED me.
6 Behold, You love truth to the core. Therefore, You have taught me wisdom in my core.

Memo Devo 2.0
Psalm 51:1-13
Subject: Love, Part 2

Day 4
Ps51:7-9

7 PURGE me with HYSSOP and I shall be clean. Wash me, and I shall be WHITER than snow.
8 MAKE me HEAR joy and gladness, so that the bones which You have broken may rejoice.
9 HIDE Your FACE from my sin and put away all my iniquities.

Steve's Mnemonic: The "_H"s (PH, WH, MH, FH) See caps ↑

Obviously, this is another very general aid. WHITER is a single word and F and H are even reversed. But again, it works for me and that's all that really matters.

We can get so overwhelmed with grief in our prayers that we forget the joy and gladness that awaits when we rest in Jesus. David somehow understands this. Even in the depths of his despair, he chooses to believe that Jesus' love is the only way back to true peace. This is also what Paul is talking about in Philippians 3_7-8 when he speaks of "counting everything as loss in view of the surpassing value of Christ Jesus". Nothing is more valuable than the redemption we have in Christ.

Put it Together Using the Tide Technique

...5 Behold, I was BORN in iniquity. And in sin has my mother CONCEIVED me.
6 Behold, You love truth to the core. Therefore, You have taught me wisdom in my core.
7 PURGE me with HYSSOP and I shall be clean. Wash me, and I shall be WHITER than snow.
8 MAKE me HEAR joy and gladness, so that the bones which You have broken may rejoice.
9 HIDE Your FACE from my sin and put away all my iniquities.

Memo Devo 2.0
Psalm 51:1-13
Subject: Love, Part 2

Day 5
Ps51:10-13

10 CREATE in me a clean heart, O God, and renew a right spirit within me.
11 CAST me not away from Your presence, and TAKE not Your Holy Spirit from me.
12 RESTORE to me the joy of Your salvation, and ESTABLISH me with Your free Spirit.
13 Then shall I TEACH Your ways to the wicked, and sinners shall be CONVERTED to You.

Steve's Mnemonics: "CTR" and "ETC"

v10 is again the famous one, so I begin with v11, where two common 21st Century abbreviations serve as acronyms for the 10th Century BC words in CAPS.

Point to Ponder

David understands that God not only has the power to forgive his sins, but that He can actually re-make him into a completely new creation, totally unconnected to his past mistakes. This is echoed in Paul's 2nd letter to the church at Corinth 1000 years later (2Corinthians 5:17). But MOST importantly, David understands that the ultimate purpose of such redemption is not to benefit him, but to magnify God.

Put it Together Using the Tide Technique*

...10 CREATE in me a clean heart, O God, and renew a right spirit within me.
11 CAST me not away from Your presence and TAKE not Your Holy Spirit from me.
12 RESTORE to me the joy of Your salvation and ESTABLISH me with Your free Spirit.
13 Then shall I TEACH Your ways to the wicked, and sinners shall be CONVERTED to You.

*I take the weekend to slowly "tide back" one verse at a time, until I have incorporated everything and can speak vv1-13 back to at least one other person without the text.

Also available from Steve Cook:
https://www.5talentsaudio.com

Memo Devo: Memorization as Devotion
8 Devotionals Designed to Help You Begin to Activate More Scripture in your Life

What if there was a way to experience more of God's power in my life and be a more effective witness for God, using only the time and resources I already possess? I'd have an inexpensive way to achieve two of my main spiritual goals: better intimacy with God and a better witness for God. Since I started memorizing long passages of Scripture in 2009, I have drawn closer than ever to Jesus and gained new peace and confidence in sharing the Gospel. This first volume in the Memo Devo series is designed to help you do the same thing and begin to activate more Scripture in your life so that you can love Jesus better than you ever have before. Just as He promised. (John 15:7-8, 17:17)

WTB_Mark
A Living and Active Stage Adaptation of Mark's Gospel

Based on Steve's much-acclaimed audio recording, "Witness The Bible: Mark", this experimental stage adaptation of Mark's Gospel in two Acts contains a cinematic underscore of music and sound effects, over which the action is meticulously timed out. The result is a powerful activation of God's Word. It is prop-less with a very simple set and costumes and runs about 90 minutes with one intermission. It is designed to replicate what Bible study must have been like in the 1st Century Church, when most believers were illiterate.

*"The children see Jesus through Steve.
The love he has for Him really shines through."*

-Rosalyn Johnston, Discipleship Coordinator, Perimeter Church, Atlanta GA

*"From the moment I met Steve
his incredible giftings were quite evident.
A master of character voices,
his servant's heart shines through in every situation."*

-Frank Montenegro, Voice of Dr. Kendall Park, Creationworks' 'Jonathan Park'

*"Steve is gifted in ways most actors are not.
And to know that he is using his talents
to glorify the Word and the Lord
are inspiring to me."*

-Brad Sherrill, Actor, The Gospel of John

*"Steve makes the Scriptures real
in ways most folks haven't experienced before.
As one woman said immediately afterwards,
'I've been part of some wonderful worship experiences before, but
nothing as powerful as that!'"*

Jeff Jansen, Pastor, Dunwoody Community Church, Atlanta

For booking and Press inquiries, please call Steve at 404.579.6864

"That your faith should not be in the wisdom of men, but in the power of God."
1Cor2_5

www.5talentsaudio.com

©2015-2021 Five Talents Audio

www.ingramcontent.com/pod-product-compliance
Lightning Source LLC
LaVergne TN
LVHW052256070426
835507LV00035B/3047